CAST IRON

VEGETARIAN

COOKBOOK

Delectable recipes in your cast-iron and

dutch oven

SALLY SMITH

1

COPYRIGHT

TABLE OF CONTENTS

INTRODUCTION **8**

History 11

Production............................... 16

CAST IRON...............................**18**

Types of cast iron..................... 18

Benefits Of Cooking In Cast Iron For

Vegans 32

Cast Iron vs Enameled Cast
Iron(Dutch oven): Which One Is
Best?...................................... 43

Benefits Of Enameled Cast Iron .. 44

Cons of Enameled Cast Iron 45

Cast Iron Skillet 46

How To Season Cast Iron For The
First Time 47

What is the best oil to season a cast
iron skillet? 53

Is cast iron supposed to smoke when
seasoning? 55

What temperature do I season my
cast iron? 56

How often do you season a cast iron?
.... 57

How To Season A Rusty Cast Iron
Skillet 57

How To Care For Cast Iron: Guide For Beginners 58

What Not To Cook In A Cast Iron 59

RECIPES.................................63

1.   Skillet Eggplant Parm.......... 63

2.   Tomato Cobbler with Cornmeal-Cheddar Biscuits 68

3.   Santiago Salsa (Beans and Rice Dip) 75

4.   Green Shakshuka 78

5.   Upside Down Tomato Corn Cake 82

6.   Tex-Mex Migas 86

7.   Caprese Grilled Cheese 89

8.   Summer Squash Gratin 92

9.   Greek Scramble 95

10.   Spinach and Refried Bean Quesadillas.............................. 99

11.   Tofu Steak with Miso & Ginger 102

12.   Chickpea Salad with Cumin & Garlic 104

13.   Skillet Mac & Cheese 109

14.   Mexican Skillet Lasagna .. 113

15.   How To Make the Best Tomato Grilled Cheese 117

16.   Veggie Burgers 123

INTRODUCTION

Cast iron is a group of iron-carbon alloys with a carbon content more than 2%. Its usefulness derives from its relatively low melting temperature. The alloy constituents affect its colour when fractured: white cast iron has carbide impurities which allow cracks to pass straight through, grey cast iron has graphite flakes which deflect a passing crack and initiate countless new cracks as the material breaks, and ductile cast iron has spherical graphite "nodules" which stop the crack from further progressing.

Carbon (C) ranging from 1.8 to 4 wt%, and silicon (Si) 1–3 wt%, are the main alloying elements of cast iron. Iron alloys with lower carbon content are known as steel.

Cast iron tends to be brittle, except for malleable cast irons. With its relatively low melting point, good fluidity, castability, excellent machinability, resistance to deformation and wear resistance, cast irons have become an engineering material with a wide range of applications and are used in pipes, machines and automotive industry parts, such as cylinder heads, cylinder blocks and gearbox cases. It is resistant to damage by oxidation but is difficult to weld.

The earliest cast-iron artefacts date to the 5th century BC, and were discovered by archaeologists in what is now Jiangsu in China. Cast iron was used in ancient China for warfare, agriculture, and architecture. During the 15th century, cast iron became utilized for cannon in Burgundy, France, and in England during the Reformation. The amounts of cast iron used for cannon required large scale production. The first cast-iron bridge was built during the 1770s by Abraham Darby III, and is known as The Iron Bridge in

Shropshire, England. Cast iron was also used in the construction of buildings.

History

Cast iron and wrought iron can be produced unintentionally when smelting copper using iron ore as a flux.

The earliest cast-iron artifacts date to the 5th century BC, and were discovered by archaeologists in what is now modern Luhe County, Jiangsu in China during the Warring States period. This is based on an analysis of the artifact's microstructures.

Because cast iron is comparatively brittle, it is not suitable for purposes where a sharp edge or flexibility is required. It is strong under compression, but not under tension. Cast iron was invented in China in the 5th century BC and poured into molds to make ploughshares and pots as well as weapons and pagodas. Although steel was more desirable, cast iron was cheaper and thus was more commonly used for implements in ancient China, while wrought iron or steel was used for weapons. The Chinese developed a method of annealing cast iron by keeping hot castings in an oxidizing atmosphere for a week or longer in order to burn off some carbon near the surface in order to keep the surface layer from being too brittle.

In the west, where it did not become available until the 15th century, its earliest uses included cannon and shot. Henry VIII initiated the casting of cannon in England. Soon, English iron workers using blast furnaces developed the technique of producing cast-iron cannons, which, while heavier than the prevailing bronze cannons, were much cheaper and enabled England to arm her navy better. The technology of cast iron was transferred from China. Al-Qazvini in the 13th century and other travellers subsequently noted an iron industry in the Alburz Mountains to the south of the Caspian Sea. This is close to the silk route, so that the use of technology derived from China is conceivable. The ironmasters of the Weald continued producing cast irons until the 1760s, and armament was one of the main uses of irons after the Restoration.

Cast-iron pots were made at many English blast furnaces at the time. In 1707, Abraham Darby patented a new method of making pots (and kettles) thinner and hence cheaper than those made by traditional methods. This meant that his Coalbrookdale furnaces became dominant as suppliers of pots, an activity in which they were joined in the 1720s and 1730s by a small number of other coke-fired blast furnaces.

Application of the steam engine to power blast bellows (indirectly by pumping water to a waterwheel) in Britain, beginning in 1743 and increasing in the 1750s, was a key factor in increasing the production of cast iron, which surged in the following decades. In addition to overcoming the limitation on water power, the steam-pumped-water powered blast gave higher furnace temperatures, which allowed the use of higher lime ratios, enabling the conversion from charcoal, supplies of wood for which were inadequate, to coke.

Production

Cast iron is made from pig iron, which is the product of melting iron ore in a blast furnace. Cast iron can be made directly from the molten pig iron or by re-melting pig iron, often along with substantial quantities of iron, steel, limestone, carbon (coke) and taking various steps to remove undesirable contaminants. Phosphorus and sulfur may be burnt out of the molten iron, but this also burns out the carbon, which must be replaced. Depending on the application, carbon and silicon content are adjusted to the desired levels, which may be anywhere from 2–3.5% and 1–3%, respectively. If desired, other elements are then added to the melt before the final form is produced by casting.

Cast iron is sometimes melted in a special type of blast furnace known as a cupola, but in modern applications, it is more often melted in electric induction furnaces or electric arc furnaces. After melting is complete, the molten cast iron is poured into a holding furnace or ladle.

Types of cast iron

Alloying elements

Cast iron's properties are changed by adding various alloying elements, or alloyants. Next to carbon, silicon is the most important alloyant because it forces carbon out of solution. A low percentage of silicon allows carbon to remain in solution forming iron carbide and the production of white cast iron. A high percentage of silicon forces carbon out of solution forming graphite and the production of grey cast iron. Other alloying agents, manganese, chromium, molybdenum, titanium and vanadium counteracts silicon, promotes the retention of carbon, and the formation of those carbides. Nickel and copper increase strength, and machinability, but do not change the amount of graphite formed. The carbon in the form of graphite results in a softer iron, reduces shrinkage, lowers strength, and decreases density. Sulfur, largely a contaminant when present, forms iron sulfide, which prevents the formation of graphite and increases hardness. The problem with sulfur is that it makes molten cast iron viscous, which causes defects. To counter the effects of sulfur, manganese is added because the two form into manganese sulfide instead of iron sulfide. The manganese sulfide is lighter than the melt, so it tends to float out of the melt and into the slag. The amount of manganese required to neutralize sulfur is $1.7 \times$ sulfur content $+ 0.3\%$. If more than this amount of manganese is added, then manganese carbide forms, which increases hardness and chilling, except in grey iron, where up to 1% of manganese increases strength and density.

Nickel is one of the most common alloying elements because it refines the pearlite and graphite structure, improves toughness, and evens out hardness differences between section thicknesses. Chromium is added in small amounts to reduce free graphite, produce chill, and because it is a powerful carbide stabilizer; nickel is often added in conjunction. A small amount of tin can be added as a substitute for 0.5% chromium. Copper is added in the ladle or in the furnace, on the order of 0.5–2.5%, to decrease chill, refine graphite, and increase fluidity. Molybdenum is added on the order of 0.3–1% to increase chill and refine the graphite and pearlite structure; it is often added in conjunction with nickel, copper, and chromium to form high strength irons. Titanium is added as a degasser and deoxidizer, but it also increases fluidity. 0.15–0.5% vanadium is added to cast iron to stabilize cementite, increase hardness, and increase resistance to wear and heat. 0.1–0.3% zirconium helps to form graphite, deoxidize, and increase fluidity.

In malleable iron melts, bismuth is added, on the scale of 0.002–0.01%, to increase how much silicon can be added. In white iron, boron is added to aid in the production of malleable iron; it also reduces the coarsening effect of bismuth.

Grey cast iron

Grey cast iron is characterised by its graphitic microstructure, which causes fractures of the material to have a grey appearance. It is the most commonly used cast iron and the most widely used cast material based on weight. Most cast irons have a chemical composition of 2.5–4.0% carbon, 1–3% silicon, and the remainder iron. Grey cast iron has less tensile strength and shock resistance than steel, but its compressive strength is comparable to low- and medium-

23

carbon steel. These mechanical properties are controlled by the size and shape of the graphite flakes present in the microstructure and can be characterised according to the guidelines given by the ASTM.

White cast iron

White cast iron displays white fractured surfaces due to the presence of an iron carbide precipitate called cementite. With a lower silicon content (graphitizing agent) and faster cooling rate, the carbon in white cast iron precipitates out of the melt as the metastable phase cementite, Fe_3C, rather than graphite.

The cementite which precipitates from the melt forms as relatively large particles. As the iron carbide precipitates out, it withdraws carbon from the original melt, moving the mixture toward one that is closer to eutectic, and the remaining phase is the lower iron-carbon austenite (which on cooling might transform to martensite). These eutectic carbides are much too large to provide the benefit of what is called precipitation hardening (as in some steels, where much smaller cementite precipitates might inhibit [plastic deformation] by impeding the movement of dislocations through the pure iron ferrite matrix).

Rather, they increase the bulk hardness of the cast iron simply by virtue of their own very high hardness and their substantial volume fraction, such that the bulk hardness can be approximated by a rule of mixtures. In any case, they offer hardness at the expense of toughness. Since carbide makes up a large fraction of the material, white cast iron could reasonably be classified as a cermet. White iron is too brittle for use in many structural components, but with good hardness and abrasion resistance and relatively low cost, it finds use in such applications as the wear surfaces (impeller and volute) of slurry pumps, shell liners and lifter bars in ball mills and autogenous grinding mills, balls and rings in coal pulverisers, and the teeth of a backhoe's digging bucket (although cast medium-carbon martensitic steel is more common for this application).

It is difficult to cool thick castings fast enough to solidify the melt as white cast iron all the way through. However, rapid cooling can be used to solidify a shell of white cast iron, after which the remainder cools more slowly to form a core of grey cast iron. The resulting casting, called a chilled casting, has the benefits of a hard surface with a somewhat tougher interior.

27

High-chromium white iron alloys allow massive castings (for example, a 10-tonne impeller) to be sand cast, as the chromium reduces cooling rate required to produce carbides through the greater thicknesses of material. Chromium also produces carbides with impressive abrasion resistance. These high-chromium alloys attribute their superior hardness to the presence of chromium carbides. The main form of these carbides are the eutectic or primary M_7C_3 carbides, where "M" represents iron or chromium and can vary depending on the alloy's composition. The eutectic carbides form as bundles of hollow hexagonal rods and grow perpendicular to the hexagonal basal plane. The hardness of these carbides are within the range of 1500-1800HV.

Malleable cast iron

Malleable iron starts as a white iron casting that is then heat treated for a day or two at about 950 °C (1,740 °F) and then cooled over a day or two. As a result, the carbon in iron carbide transforms into graphite and ferrite plus carbon (austenite). The slow process allows the surface tension to form the graphite into spheroidal particles rather than flakes. Due to their lower aspect ratio, the spheroids are relatively short and far from one another, and have a lower cross section vis-a-vis a propagating crack or phonon. They also have blunt boundaries, as opposed to flakes, which alleviates the stress concentration problems found in grey cast iron. In general, the properties of malleable cast iron are more like those of mild steel. There is a limit to how large a part can be cast in malleable iron, as it is made from white cast iron.

Ductile cast iron

Developed in 1948, nodular or ductile cast iron has its graphite in the form of very tiny nodules with the graphite in the form of concentric layers forming the nodules. As a result, the properties of ductile cast iron are that of a spongy steel without the stress concentration effects that flakes of graphite would produce. The carbon percentage present is 3-4% and percentage of silicon is 1.8-2.8%.Tiny amounts of 0.02 to 0.1% magnesium, and only 0.02 to 0.04% cerium added to these alloys slow the growth of graphite precipitates by bonding to the edges of the graphite planes. Along with careful control of other elements and timing, this allows the carbon to separate as spheroidal particles as the material solidifies. The properties are similar to malleable iron, but parts can be cast with larger sections.

Benefits Of Cooking In Cast Iron For Vegans

Here are the numerous benefits of cooking in cast iron pans and skillets you may have never thought of.

• Non-Toxic

Cast iron cookware is made up of 97% iron and doesn't give off any toxic fumes like Teflon-coated pans. Teflon is made from PFOA's which create a great non-stick barrier on pans but they quickly wear out and need replacing.

If you continue to use a scratched or damaged Teflon-coated pan, you may be putting yourself at risk of ingesting some of the chemicals.

Also, after the pans are damaged and thrown away, the chemical coating lives on and can make its way into our drinking water supply. The EPA recommends limiting our exposure to PFOA ingestion.

- Durability

Cast iron skillets seem to last forever. Many families pass down grandma's favorite skillet as a family heirloom.

The secondary cast iron collector's market even has cast iron pieces form the early 1800's that are still good as new. Despite the age of the pan, you can restore it and cook with it even today.

They're unlikely to warp and can take a beating before cracking. After you acquire some cast iron cookware for yourself, you'll likely never have to buy another piece again.

- Extra Iron

Cooking in cast iron can add a significant amount of iron to your diet. This is great for vegans who need to get more iron into their diet.

In fact, researchers found that giving populations in third world countries that suffer from anemia a cast iron to cook with, helped prevent iron deficiency anemia.

One word of caution is that people who have hemochromatosis where they already absorb too much iron from their food should never cook in cast iron.

- Non-Stick

A cast iron that has been seasoned properly is practically non-stick.

Oil on your pan gets heated up until fat polymerization. This polymerized oil is hard and bonds to the iron, creating a nonstick surface.

With proper seasoning and regular use, cast iron gives you all of the non-stick properties you're looking for without the over-engineered chemicals.

- Easy Cleaning

Often, with stainless steel, food sticks unless you use a lot of oil. Once it sticks, it's tough to get the burnt food off without hours of soaking and elbow grease.

Once your cast iron has been seasoned, there won't be much food that sticks to your pan. Unless you overheat the cast iron or cook really acidic foods, your pan should clean up with a quick scrub.

- Oven Safe

Cast iron can move from the stove to the oven to the fire. As long as your piece doesn't have a wooden handle or other style knobs, you're able to make a one-pan meal where you start on the stovetop and finish it in the oven.

- Low Oil Cooking Possible

It may sound counterintuitive that you can cook low-oil in cast iron when you need oil in order to get the non-stick finish.

Once the seasoning is built up, you can cook dishes with very little oil, sometimes no oil at all. Just make sure you wipe a little oil on your cast iron before you put it away so that it stays protected and prevents rust.

You don't need to worry about the seasoning transferring oil to your dishes either. Once the oil is polymerized, it only wears off in minute amounts.

- Less Waste

If you're used to non-stick coated pans, chances are, you're familiar with buying new ones every few months. Over time, the coating wears off or gets damaged, rendering it dangerous to continue using.

If you go through two pans a year for over 30 years, that's 60 pans in the landfill for one person. This really adds up if you have multiple non-stick kitchenware that needs to be replaced.

Cooking with cast iron is the eco-choice and will save you lots of money in the long run. While a brand new cast iron

39

skillet may cost you more than a cheap non-stick pan, picking a cast iron pan up at the thrift store is the most economical way to go.

- Energy Efficient

Cast iron is a poor conductor of heat. This means that it holds onto heat and the temperature isn't easily changed. Contrast this to copper pans where you can raise and lower the temperature on the stovetop quickly.

Because of this, cast iron requires preheating but once it's heated, it'll hold onto that heat and keep your food evenly warm. In order to achieve this even heating and avoid hotspots, make sure you give your cast iron 15-20 minutes to heat up before using it.

- Able To Use Metal Utensils

With the rise in popularity of chemical non-stick pans, soft nylon and silicon utensils became essential so as not to damage the pans.

Bare cast iron is tough. Metal utensils hold up longer and won't get melted like plastic ones or wear out fast like silicone. You can rest easy and use your metal utensils with cast iron because it can handle it.

Please note that metal utensils shouldn't be used with enameled cast iron since the enamel coating could chip.

- Makes You Stronger

Cast iron is heavy which is typically a detractor for using it. A 10 inch cast iron skillet weighs an average of 5 lbs.

This makes them sturdy and stable for cooking but not great for recipes where you have to flip or lift up the pan.

For instance, if you wanted to cook authentic stir-fry in a wok, I'd go for a carbon steel wok rather than the 12 lb cast iron version.

Regularly lifting cast iron pans and pots will help build up your muscles. Just make sure you can handle it before you have a hot skillet in your hands.

Cast Iron vs Enameled Cast Iron(Dutch oven): Which One Is Best?

Uncoated cast iron is good for just about everything except its kryptonite, acidic foods. Cooking acidic foods like tomato sauce in an uncoated cast iron can strip your seasoning and impart a metallic taste to your food.

Acidic foods cooked in cast iron can increase the food's iron content 6 times or more depending on how long it's cooked for.

Benefits Of Enameled Cast Iron

Enameled cast iron has many benefits. It's a great option for someone who wants a little less maintenance or if you cook alkaline/acidic dishes.

- Can cook acidic foods in it.

- Doesn't require seasoning.

- Comes in lots of colors rather than black iron.

- Will not rust.

Cons of Enameled Cast Iron

There are some detractors of enameled cast iron. Having a combination of both uncoated and enameled cast iron gives you the best of both worlds.

The porcelain glass enamel coating can become damaged if dropped.

Must use wooden, silicone, or nylon cooking utensils so you don't scratch the enamel.

Food sticks at hight heat so better off with lower cooking temperatures.

Preheating an enameled cast iron cookware too hot can damage it.

Especially important to note if you intend to sear at high heat.

Cast Iron Skillet

Between a 9 inch and 13.25 inch cast iron skillet is a good place to start. The 9 inch is great for making cornbread or cooking for one.

A 10.25-inch skillet is the perfect size for baking cakes. My most used skillet size is the 12-inch skillet. It's large enough to make dinners for the family but not too large where I don't want to lift it.

How To Season Cast Iron For The First Time

No matter whether you got your cast iron brand new or second hand, you're going to want to clean and season it. Yes, even preseasoned cast iron needs to be seasoned.

Often the factory preseasoning is uneven and not as nonstick. You don't need to remove the factory seasoning, just add to it to make it even better.

There's also no telling what has happened to the pans traveling from the

47

factory to the store or in the years it was used by someone else.

- Wash & Dry Your Cast Iron

Preheat your oven to 200 degrees. Remove any labels or stickers from your cast iron. Wash it with warm soapy water and towel dry.

- Initial Bake

Once your oven is preheated and your cast iron is washed/dried, put it into the 200 degree oven for 20 minutes.

- Oil Liberally

After 20 minutes is up, wear heat protecting gloves while you remove your cast iron from the oven. Leave the oven on.

Once it's out, oil it liberally with Crisco All-Vegetable Shortening. Yes, the same Crisco in a can you grew up with.

- Remove As Much Oil As Possible

Use another lint-free towel to try to wipe out as much oil as you can. Wipe like you made a mistake and now want no oil in the pan.

It may seem counterintuitive to try to wipe away the oil after having just applied it but this keeps your seasoning layer from being too thick and flaking.

Don't worry, there will still be plenty of oil leftover in your pan for seasoning. The most common mistake of seasoning is too much oil.

- Place Cast Iron Back In The Oven

Once oiled, place the cast iron back into the 200 degree oven upside down. You may want to place a baking sheet or foil on the rack beneath the cast iron to catch excess oil that drips.

Change the temperature to 300 degrees. Once your oven reaches 300 degrees, remove the cast iron with heat-safe gloves or oven mitts. Continue to leave the oven on.

Wipe it out again with a towel to remove as much oil as possible. This step makes sure all excess oil has been removed.

Having too much oil creates spots and flakey seasoning in your cast iron. Less is more.

- Seasoning Bake

Place the cast iron back into the 300 degree oven upside down. Now increase the temperature to 450 degrees.

Once the temperature reaches 450 degrees, set your timer for one hour. Allow your cast iron to cook for the entire hour.

It may get a little smokey so make sure you have your vent fans on so you don't set off smoke alarms.

- Cooling Off

After the hour is up, avoid opening up the oven. Simply turn the oven off and allow your cast iron to remain in the oven until it cools down completely.

If you don't have time for this or want to do a second seasoning coating more quickly, at least wait until the oven has cooled down to 200 degrees before taking the cast iron out.

- Do A Second & Third Coat

A second and third seasoning coat will give you a well-seasoned pan. For these coats, start back at step 3 and avoid the initial soap/water cleaning.

Once complete, your pan may look light brown or gray. Don't worry, that's completely normal. The more you cook with high fat foods in your cast iron, the darker black your pan will get.

What is the best oil to season a cast iron skillet?

I use and recommend vegetable shortening (Crisco) to season a cast iron skillet. The initial seasoning that creates the non-stick coating does best with a vegetable oil like shortening or canola oil.

Olive oil, avocado oil, and coconut oil are great to cook with but not for the initial seasoning. Low smoke point oils are problematic in creating a good seasoning coat.

Another popular seasoning oil is flaxseed oil. I initially used this to season my cast iron but I found it to eventually create a lot of flakes on my pans.

After scrubbing out the pans and re-seasoning them with vegetable shortening, I haven't had this issue. Flaxseed oil is much more expensive and requires 5-6 coats to get a similar seasoning of 3 coats of vegetable shortening.

Is cast iron supposed to smoke when seasoning?

What oil you used during the seasoning process will determine how much smoke is produced. Your oven is set no higher than 450 degrees for seasoning but many oils' smoke points are lower than this.

The smoke point of vegetable shortening is around 360 degrees but the Crisco brand vegetable shortening says it can go up to 490 degrees.

Flaxseed oil's smoke point is 450 degrees. Other plant oils have much lower smoke points and aren't recommended for the seasoning process.

Make sure you keep your above stove vent fans on or open some windows to help with the air flow.

What temperature do I season my cast iron?

Season a cast iron with vegetable shortening at 450 degrees for one hour. Let it cool down in the oven. Repeat the seasoning process two to three times.

How often do you season a cast iron?

If your pan has been seasoned correctly, it shouldn't have to go through another seasoning. Frequent use and cooking with oils deposits additional seasoning automatically.

You may need to go through a re-seasoning process again if you're having food sticking issues or flakey seasoning.

How To Season A Rusty Cast Iron Skillet

If your cast iron skillet is rusty, it can still be seasoned. It simply requires a little bit more prep work before going through the steps.

How To Care For Cast Iron: Guide For Beginners

Cast iron requires some maintenance and care in order to keep the seasoning layer in tip-top shape.

• After you're done cooking and your pan is still warm, scrape off any food residue and rinse in warm water.

• For really stuck-on food, lightly use a chainmail scrub so you don't remove your seasoning.

• Dry your pan on low heat and then coat with a thin layer of oil. Make sure your pan is completely dry before oiling or you'll get rust.

- Store in a cool dry place until ready to use again. If you're stacking pans, place a cloth between each pan to protect the finish.

What Not To Cook In A Cast Iron

While cast iron is versatile enough for almost all cooking situations, there are a few times where uncoated cast iron isn't the best.

Long-Simmering Acidic Dishes

Cast iron doesn't do well with long-simmering acidic dishes. The longer you cook acidic foods in them, the more iron it'll leach into your food giving it a metallic taste.

A well-seasoned cast iron skillet should be fine cooking tomatoes or lemon dishes for 15 minutes or so. It was only after 30 minutes of simmering tomato sauce that taste testers were able to detect a distinct metallic taste.

But if simmering homemade tomato sauce is what you love doing, use an enameled cast iron dutch oven instead. The enamel is the protective seasoning and doesn't wear away with acid.

Super Sticky Foods (at first)

One of the major touted benefits of cast iron is it's nonstick coating. People often get frustrated that after going through the seasoning process food still sometimes sticks.

Part of the problem is that while the pan is seasoned, some foods are a lot more sticky than others. Until you've used your pan for a while and build up a seasoning from frequent use, it's recommended to stay away from making dishes that have a tendency to stick.

Smelly Foods

Even if you clean your cast iron pan properly, there still may be the slightest residual odor from that spicy curry you made.

This isn't usually a problem if you make a lot of savory foods. It comes more into play when you want to use the same skillet for both curry and vanilla cake.

If you like baking desserts in cast iron, you may want to pick up a second skillet just for baking. That way you won't ever have to worry about your sweet dessert smelling faintly like last night's dinner.

Another option to get rid of lingering smells is to pop your cast iron in a 400 degree oven for around 10 minutes.

RECIPES

1.   Skillet Eggplant Parm

This twist on eggplant Parmesan is no less delicious than the original and happens to be so much easier to make. It also skips the frying to make it more wholesome.

INGREDIENTS

- 1 cup fresh or panko breadcrumbs

- 3 tablespoons olive oil, divided

- 2 cloves garlic, minced

- 1/2 teaspoon kosher salt, plus more for seasoning

- 1/2 teaspoon finely chopped fresh oregano

- Pinch red pepper flakes

- 1 (28-ounce) can crushed tomatoes

- 4 small eggplants (about 1 1/2 pounds total), halved lengthwise

- 8 ounces fresh mozzarella cheese, torn into bite-sized pieces

- 1/3 cup grated Parmesan cheese

- 2 tablespoons coarsely chopped fresh basil leaves

INSTRUCTIONS

• Arrange a rack in the top third of the oven and heat to 400°F.

• Place the breadcrumbs, 1 tablespoon of oil, and a pinch of salt in a small bowl and stir to combine; set aside.

• Heat 1 tablespoon of oil in an ovenproof 12-inch skillet over medium-low heat until shimmering. Add the garlic, 1/2 teaspoon salt, oregano, and pepper flakes and sauté until fragrant, about 30 seconds.

• Stir in the tomatoes. Increase the heat to high to bring to a simmer.

65

Reduce the heat to medium-low and simmer until it just begins to thicken, about 5 minutes. Meanwhile, place the eggplant halves in a large bowl. Drizzle with the remaining 1 tablespoon of oil, sprinkle with a big pinch of salt, and toss to coat evenly.

- When the sauce is ready, nestle the eggplant halves in it cut-side down. Cover and place in the oven to bake until the top of the eggplants look collapsed and puckered, and the flesh is tender when pierced with a knife, 20 to 25 minutes.

- Remove the skillet from the oven and heat the broiler. Carefully flip over each eggplant half to be cut-side up. Spoon a little of the sauce over each half, then top evenly with the mozzarella. Sprinkle the breadcrumbs and grated Parmesan evenly over the top.

- Return the skillet to the oven and broil uncovered until the cheese is melted and bubbly and the breadcrumbs are golden-brown, 3 to 4 minutes. Sprinkle with the basil and serve immediately.

RECIPE NOTES

Storage: Leftovers can be stored in an airtight container in the refrigerator for up to 3 days.

2. Tomato Cobbler with Cornmeal-Cheddar Biscuits

Not all cobblers have to be sweet. Case in point? This delectable tomato cobbler topped with cheesy biscuits. And because this is made in a cast iron pan, you can bring it directly to the table for serving and know it'll stay pretty warm throughout the meal.

INGREDIENTS

- 3 1/2 to 4 pounds cherry tomatoes

- 1/2 tablespoon olive oil

- 2 medium red onions, peeled and thinly sliced

- 1 1/2 teaspoons salt, divided

- 4 cloves garlic, minced

- 1/4 cup red wine (or 2 tablespoons balsamic vinegar)

- 1/4 cup all-purpose flour

For the biscuits:

- 1 1/4 cups all-purpose flour

- 3/4 cup cornmeal

- 1 tablespoon baking powder

- 1/2 teaspoon baking soda

- 1/2 teaspoon salt

- 6 tablespoons cold unsalted butter

- 1 1/2 cups grated cheddar cheese, divided

- 3/4 to 1 cup buttermilk, plus extra for brushing

INSTRUCTIONS

- Heat the oven to 375°F with a rack placed in the middle of the oven.

- Pick the stems off of the cherry tomatoes and rinse them under running water. Larger tomatoes can be sliced in half, but I generally just leave the tomatoes whole.

- Warm the olive oil in a 12-inch cast iron or high-sided stainless steel skillet over medium-high heat. When warm, add the onions and 1/2 teaspoon of salt. Sauté until the onions are very soft and tender, at least 10 minutes, or if you have the patience, lower the heat and continue cooking for another 20 or 30 minutes to caramelize the onions. (Read more: How To Caramelize Onions.)

- Stir the garlic into the onions and cook until fragrant, 30 to 60 seconds. Pour in the wine (or balsamic) and cook until the wine has mostly evaporated. Stir in the flour and cook until the flour is paste-like. Remove the pan from heat.

Stir in the cherry tomatoes and 1 teaspoon of salt, carefully stirring and folding until the onions are evenly mixed with the tomatoes.

• To prepare the biscuits, combine the flour, cornmeal, baking powder, baking soda, and salt in the bowl of a food processor. Pulse a few times to combine. Cut the cold butter into chunks and scatter it over the flour. Pulse a few times until the butter has been cut into pea-sized pieces.

• Transfer the flour-and-butter mixture to a bowl and stir in 1 cup of the cheddar (reserve the other 1/2 cup for sprinkling over the top). Form a well in the middle and pour in 3/4 cup of buttermilk for firmer biscuits, or 1 cup of buttermilk for looser biscuits. Use a spatula to gently stir the buttermilk into the flour; continue stirring until all the buttermilk has been incorporated and no more dry flour remains. (Alternatively, you can make the biscuits entirely in a bowl and use your fingers or a pastry cutter to cut in the butter.)

• Drop the dough over the tomatoes, making 7 to 8 biscuits. Brush the biscuits with a little buttermilk. Place the skillet on a baking sheet to catch drips, and then transfer to the oven.

- Cook for 55 to 60 minutes, until the tomatoes are very bubbly and the tops of the biscuits are nicely browned. About 10 minutes before the end of baking, sprinkle the tops of the biscuits with the remaining 1/2 cup of cheddar.

- Remove from the oven and let the cobbler rest for at least 15 minutes before eating. Leftovers will keep for about a week.

RECIPE NOTES

This recipe can also be cooked in a 13x9-inch baking dish or other 3-quart baking dish. Prepare the tomato mixture in a skillet on the stovetop, then transfer to

the baking dish, top with the biscuits,
and bake until bubbly.

3. Santiago Salsa (Beans and Rice Dip)

While this might have originally been
thought of as a side dish or appetizer,
this bean and rice dip has enough
nutritional value to be dinner. Serve it
with a big side salad and a handful of
your favorite chips and call it a meal.

INGREDIENTS

For the dip:

- 1 (15-ounce) can pinto beans,
rinsed and drained

- 1 (15-ounce) can black beans, rinsed and drained

- 1 (15-ounce) can navy beans, rinsed and drained

- 1 cup cooked white rice

- 1 cup diced tomato

- 1/2 cup diced onion

- 3 cups (12 ounces) grated cheddar-Monterey Jack blend, divided

- 2 tablespoons finely diced pickled jalapeño

- 1/2 teaspoon ground cumin

- 1/2 teaspoon garlic powder

- 1/8 teaspoon cayenne pepper (optional)

- Kosher salt and freshly ground pepper

For serving:

- Tortilla chips

- Sour cream

- Salsa

INSTRUCTIONS

- Preheat oven to 400°.

- In a large bowl, combine the beans, rice, tomato, onion, 2 cups of cheese, jalapeno, and spices. Season

generously with kosher salt and pepper.
Pour into a greased 10-inch cast iron
skillet or round baking dish. Cover with
aluminum foil and cook for 30 minutes.

• Remove from the oven and take off
the aluminum foil. Sprinkle the
remaining 1 cup of cheese over the top
and continue to bake until the cheese is
melted, about 5 - 10 more minutes.

• Serve warm with tortilla chips, sour
cream, and salsa.

4. Green Shakshuka

Shakshuka is one of those versatile
recipes that can be served for any meal
of the day. Our green version replaces

the tomatoes with Swiss chard, spinach, and plenty of leeks.

INGREDIENTS

- 1 tablespoon olive oil

- 2 large leeks, halved lengthwise and thinly sliced

- 1 large celery stalk, sliced

- 3 garlic cloves, minced

- 1 spicy chile pepper (any variety would work here), sliced

- 1 bunch of Swiss chard, cut into 1/2-inch ribbons

- 1 cup spinach (tightly packed)

- 1/2 bunch dried oregano

- 1 teaspoon ground cumin

- Salt and pepper, to season

- 1/4 cup crumbled feta cheese

- 4 large eggs

INSTRUCTIONS

- Preheat oven to 375°F.

- Over medium heat, warm the olive oil in a 9-inch cast iron skillet. Add the sliced leeks and celery. Cook until leeks soften, about 5 minutes. Add the minced garlic and sliced spicy pepper, and sauté for another 3 minutes. Toss in the Swiss chard, spinach, oregano, and cumin.

Season to taste with salt and pepper (make sure not to over-salt the mixture, as the feta adds saltiness as well).

• Once the Swiss chard and spinach have wilted, scrape down the sides, and pat down the mixture. Sprinkle the crumbled feta over the greens mixture and carefully crack the eggs over the top, one at a time and spaced slightly apart. Add some more freshly ground black pepper.

• Transfer the skillet to the oven and bake for 7 to 10 minutes (longer if you prefer your eggs cooked more, or less time for runnier eggs). Serve

immediately with fresh crusty bread.

5. Upside Down Tomato Corn Cake

Think of this like a fancy take on

cornbread, but one that works for dinner.

All you need is a simple salad of greens

and a light dressing to go alongside.

INGREDIENTS

- 1 1/2 pints cherry tomatoes, halved

- 1 1/4 cups yellow cornmeal

- 3/4 cup all-purpose flour

- 1 tablespoon granulated sugar

- 2 teaspoons baking powder

- 1/2 teaspoon baking soda

- 1 teaspoon kosher salt

- 1/8 teaspoon freshly ground black pepper

- 2 large eggs

- 1 cup buttermilk

- 6 tablespoons unsalted butter, melted and cooled

- 1 cup fresh corn kernels (from 2 ears)

INSTRUCTIONS

- Arrange a rack in the middle of the oven and heat to 400°F. Cut out a round of parchment and line the bottom of a 10-inch cast iron skillet.

- Place the tomatoes in a single layer, cut-side up, on the parchment to cover the entire skillet.

- Whisk the cornmeal, flour, sugar, baking powder, baking soda, salt, and pepper together in a large bowl; set aside. Place the eggs, buttermilk, and butter in a medium bowl and whisk until blended. Make a well in the center of the dry ingredients. Pour in the liquid ingredients, then stir with a wooden spoon or rubber spatula just until the ingredients are combined. Fold in the corn.

• Pour the batter into the skillet, then smooth it into an even layer over the tomatoes. Bake until the top is golden-brown and the edges have pulled away from the sides of the skillet, 22 to 25 minutes.

• Let the cake cool for at least 10 minutes, then run a knife along the edge of the pan. Invert the cake onto a large plate and carefully remove the layer of parchment. Serve hot or at room temperature, sliced into wedges.

6.   Tex-Mex Migas

This tortilla-filled egg dish is another one that can be served at any meal, and it's easy to toss together with items you likely already have in your fridge and pantry.

INGREDIENTS

- 2 tablespoons olive oil

- 2/3 cup diced onion (about 1 small)

- 2 jalapeño peppers, seeded and minced

- Salt and pepper

- 4 corn tortillas, cut or torn into 1/2-inch pieces

- 8 large eggs

- 1/4 cup salsa

- 1 cup shredded cheddar or Monterey Jack cheese

- Garnish and serving options: Salsa, pico de gallo, cheese, sour cream, avocado, cilantro, scallions, corn or flour tortillas, beans

INSTRUCTIONS

- Heat the oil in a large cast iron or nonstick skillet over medium heat until shimmering. Add the onion and jalapeños, season with salt and pepper, and cook until the onion is soft and translucent. Meanwhile, place the eggs and salsa in a medium bowl, season with salt and pepper, and whisk to combine; set aside.

• When the onion is ready, add the tortillas and cook, stirring frequently, until soft, 1 to 2 minutes.

• Reduce the heat to low and add the eggs. Scramble until eggs are almost set, then fold in the cheese and remove from heat. Garnish and serve immediately.

7.   Caprese Grilled Cheese

Cast iron pans were practically made for fancy grilled cheese sandwiches — helping them get all nice and crispy on the outside as the cheese melts into a dream inside. This pesto, tomato, and mozzarella version will make you a culinary hero in your family.

INGREDIENTS

- 8 (1/2-inch thick) slices sourdough bread (from a 9-inch round boule)

- 1/4 cup basil pesto

- 8 ounces fresh mozzarella cheese, cut into 1/4-inch-thick slices

- 2 large tomatoes, cut into 1/4-inch-thick slices

- 2 tablespoons olive oil

INSTRUCTIONS

- Heat a large skillet or flat-top griddle over medium heat. Meanwhile, arrange a rack in the middle of the oven and heat to 250°F.

- Spread the pesto on one side of each slice of bread. Evenly distribute the mozzarella over 4 of the pesto bread slices, then top with the tomatoes. Top the stacks with the remaining 4 bread slices, pesto-side down.

- Brush the olive oil evenly on the outsides of the sandwiches. Place the sandwiches (2 if you're using a large skillet and all 4 if you're using a flat-top griddle large enough to fit all of them) cheese-side down in the pan. Cook until the bottom is toasted and golden-brown, about 2 minutes.

- Use a flat spatula to gently press down on each sandwich. Flip and cook until the second side is toasted and golden-brown, about 2 minutes more.

- Place the sandwiches on a baking sheet and transfer to the oven. (Repeat with cooking the remaining 2 sandwiches if you weren't able to fit them all in the pan during the first round.) Once all the sandwiches are in the oven, bake until the cheese is melted in all 4 sandwiches, about 5 to 7 minutes.

8.   Summer Squash Gratin

For any lingering zucchini and summer squash, try making this layered gratin. It's warm, cheesy, and filled with breadcrumbs. It's the perfect transitional dish as summer fades into fall.

INGREDIENTS

- 4 tablespoons olive oil, divided

- 3/4 cup panko breadcrumbs

- 1/2 cup grated Parmesan cheese

- 2 medium shallots, thinly sliced

- 2 cloves garlic, minced

- 2 pounds summer squash, cut crosswise into 1/4-inch pieces

- 1 tablespoon fresh thyme leaves

- Finely grated zest from 1/2 lemon

- 1/2 teaspoon kosher salt

- Freshly ground black pepper

INSTRUCTIONS

- Arrange a rack in the middle of the oven and heat to to 400°F. Place 2 tablespoons of the oil, panko, and

Parmesan in a medium bowl and mix to combine; set aside.

•	Heat the remaining 2 tablespoons oil in a 6- to 8-inch oven-safe frying pan or skillet over medium heat until shimmering. Add the shallots and cook, stirring occasionally, until soft and fragrant, 3 to 4 minutes. Add the garlic and cook for 1 minute more.

•	Remove the pan from the heat and add the squash, thyme, lemon zest, and salt. Season with pepper, stir to combine, and spread into an even layer. Sprinkle the panko mixture evenly over the squash.

- Transfer the skillet to the oven and bake until the top is golden-brown, 25 to 30 minutes. Let cool for about 5 minutes before serving.

9. Greek Scramble

Scrambled eggs will always be appropriate for dinner in our book. And this Greek-inspired version with spinach, feta cheese, and tomatoes is made even better by the pita triangles served on the side.

INGREDIENTS

- 10 large eggs

- 2/3 cup crumbled feta cheese

- 1/4 cup milk (not nonfat)

- 1/2 teaspoon fine salt, plus more for seasoning

- 1/4 teaspoon freshly ground black pepper, plus more for seasoning

- 1 tablespoon olive oil

- 1/2 medium yellow onion, diced

- 5 to 6 ounces baby spinach

- 1 cup cherry tomatoes, quartered

- Toast or toasted pita bread, for serving

INSTRUCTIONS

•   Whisk the eggs, feta, milk, 1/2 teaspoon salt, and 1/4 teaspoon pepper in a large bowl to combine; set aside.

•   Heat the oil in a large nonstick frying pan or seasoned cast iron skillet over medium heat until shimmering. Add the onion, season with salt, and cook, stirring occasionally, until softened, about 5 minutes. Add the spinach, tossing continually, until completely wilted and any liquid has evaporated, about 3 minutes.

•   Reduce the heat to medium-low and pour in the egg mixture. Let sit undisturbed until the eggs just start to set around the edges, 1 to 2 minutes. Using a rubber spatula, push the set eggs from the edges into the center. Spread the uncooked eggs back into an even layer. Repeat, pushing the set eggs from the edges into the center every 30 seconds until almost set, for a total cooking time of about 5 to 6 minutes. (The top of the eggs should still be slightly wet.)

• Remove the pan from the heat and fold in the tomatoes. Serve immediately with toast or toasted pita bread.

10. Spinach and Refried Bean Quesadillas

We tend to forget about quesadillas, but these are so easy to make that when we remember, we incorporate them into our dinner routine weekly. Using refried beans instead of canned black beans makes them easy to assemble and even easier to eat. Making them in a cast iron pan is a sure ticket to a crispy exterior.

INGREDIENTS

- 1 tablespoon olive oil

- 1 (5- to 6-ounce) bag baby spinach

- 1 clove garlic, finely chopped

99

- 1/2 teaspoon chili powder

- Salt

- 4 large (9- to 10-inch) flour tortillas

- 1 cup vegetarian refried beans

- 2 cups shredded Monterey Jack cheese or Monterey Jack and cheddar cheese blend

- Optional toppings: Salsa, guacamole, sour cream, Mexican hot sauce

INSTRUCTIONS

- Heat the oil in a large frying pan (at least 10 inches) over medium-high heat until shimmering. Add the spinach and garlic and cook, stirring often, until just wilted, about 3 minutes. Add the chili powder, season lightly with salt, and cook until all the visible liquid is evaporated, about 2 minutes more. Transfer the spinach to a fine-mesh strainer and use the back of a wooden spoon or a ladle to press out as much liquid as possible; set the spinach aside.

• Assemble the quesadillas: Place the tortillas on a work surface. Spread 1/4 cup of the beans over half of each tortilla. Divide the cheese over the beans, pressing the cheese gently into the beans. Divide the spinach over the cheese. Fold each tortilla in half so the empty side covers the filling.

• Wipe out the frying pan with paper towels and place back over medium heat until hot, about 3 minutes. Add 2 of the quesadillas and cook until golden-brown on the outside and the cheese is melted, about 3 minutes per side. Remove to a cutting board and repeat with the remaining quesadillas. Cut the quesadillas into wedges and serve with toppings.

11. Tofu Steak with Miso & Ginger

Of course your cast iron pan is perfect for cooking tofu, and this ginger-miso recipe is a prime candidate. Just make sure the pan is well-seasoned so your tofu doesn't stick.

INGREDIENTS

- 1 (14-ounce) block extra firm tofu

- 1 tablespoon white miso

- 6 tablespoons warm water

- 3 tablespoons finely grated ginger

- Vegetable oil for frying

- Scallions and sesame seeds for garnish (optional)

INSTRUCTIONS

- Drain and rinse tofu. Cut into 6 slices. Place tofu slices between clean kitchen towels (or paper towels) on a dish or cutting board. Gently press to remove excess water.

- In a small bowl, mix together miso, water, and ginger.

12. Chickpea Salad with Cumin & Garlic

This recipe starts with cooking cumin and red pepper flakes in a bit of hot oil before the chickpeas are added in. You can serve this dish warm out of the pan and enjoy it chilled the next day.

INGREDIENTS

- 3 tablespoons olive oil

- 2 tablespoons whole cumin seeds

- 1/4 teaspoon dried red pepper flakes, or to taste

- 4 garlic cloves, finely minced

- 2 15-ounce cans chickpeas (garbanzo beans), rinsed and drained

- 1/2 cup oil-packed sun-dried tomatoes, drained and finely chopped

- 3/4 cup Italian parsley, leaves only

- Small handful fresh mint leaves

- 1 lemon, zested and juiced

- 3/4 pound English cucumber

- Flaky sea salt

INSTRUCTIONS

- Heat the olive oil in a heavy skillet (cast iron is nice) over medium heat. When the oil is hot, add the cumin seeds and crushed red pepper and cook over medium heat, stirring constantly, for about one minute or until the seeds are toasted. The cumin will turn slightly darker in color, and smell toasty.

- Turn the heat to medium low and add the garlic. Cook, stirringly frequently, for about three minutes or until the garlic is turning golden. Do not let it scorch or turn brown.

- Add the drained chickpeas and the chopped tomatoes and turn the heat up to medium high. Cook, stirring frequently, until the chickpeas are warmed through and are shiny with oil. Turn off the heat.

- Strip any remaining stems away from the Italian parsley. Finely mince the parsley and the mint and toss this with the chickpeas. Stir the lemon juice and zest into the chickpeas.

- Peel the cucumber and cut it in half lengthwise. Scrape out (and discard) the seeds with the tip of a teaspoon or grapefruit spoon. Dice the cucumber into small, 1/2-inch square cubes. Toss the cucumber with the chickpeas. Taste for salt. If necessary, add flaky sea salt to taste.

• Refrigerate for at least an hour before eating. This salad is best after it has had a chance to sit overnight in the fridge, letting its spices and juices soak together into more than the sum of its parts. Serve slightly warm or room temperature. Really good at any temperature, actually.

13. Skillet Mac & Cheese

The beauty of this mac and cheese recipe is that you only need to use one pan — your cast iron one. That means you can have delicious, creamy comfort food without a ton of dishes. We call that a win-win situation.

INGREDIENTS

•   8 ounces dried jumbo elbow macaroni, conchiglie, or pipette pasta

•   4 tablespoons unsalted butter

•   1 cup panko or other breadcrumbs

•   1 teaspoon coarsely chopped fresh thyme leaves

- 3 tablespoons all-purpose flour

- 1 1/2 cups whole milk

- 1 1/2 cups grated sharp cheddar cheese

- 1 teaspoon Dijon mustard

- 1/4 teaspoon kosher salt

- 1/8 teaspoon paprika

INSTRUCTIONS

- Arrange a rack in the middle of the oven and heat to 400°F. Meanwhile, bring a large pot of salted water to a boil. Add the pasta and cook per package instructions until al dente. Drain and set aside.

- Melt the butter in a 9- or 10-inch cast iron skillet over medium heat. Remove 1 tablespoon of the butter and combine with the breadcrumbs and thyme in a small bowl; set aside.

- Sprinkle the flour evenly into the skillet and whisk until fragrant, 1 to 2 minutes. Slowly add the milk while whisking to ensure it doesn't clump. Switch to a wooden spoon and continue cooking the sauce, stirring constantly, until it has noticeably thickened and coats the back of the spoon, 2 to 3 minutes.

- Remove the skillet from the heat and stir the cheese into the sauce, one handful at a time, until melted and smooth. Stir in mustard, salt, and paprika. Add the cooked pasta and stir gently until the pasta and sauce are evenly combined. Sprinkle the breadcrumbs evenly over top.

- Transfer the skillet to the oven and bake until the sauce is bubbling and the top is golden-brown, 10 to 15 minutes.

RECIPE NOTES

Storage: Leftovers can be stored in an airtight container in the refrigerator for up to 4 days.

14. Mexican Skillet Lasagna

Think of this somewhere between enchiladas and lasagna — it's layered with plenty of sauce, cheese, beans, soyrizo, and veggies, but instead of noodles you'll use tortillas.

INGREDIENTS

•   8 ounces fresh Mexican chorizo or soyrizo, casings removed

•   2 (12-ounce) containers salsa (3 cups)

•   1 1/2 cups low-sodium chicken or vegetable broth

- 1 (15-ounce) can black beans, drained and rinsed

- 8 ounces (about 10) dry lasagna noodles

- 1 1/2 cups shredded Monterey Jack or Mexican blend cheese

- Coarsely chopped cilantro, for garnishing (optional)

INSTRUCTIONS

- Heat a large regular or cast iron skillet (at least 12 inches wide) over medium heat. Add in the chorizo and cook, breaking the meat up into small pieces with a wooden spoon, until cooked through, about 4 minutes.

• Add the salsa, broth, and beans; stir to combine; and bring to a simmer. Using your hands, break the lasagna noodles into 1 1/2- to 2-inch pieces and add to the skillet. Stir to combine and spread into an even layer, making sure as many of the noodles are submerged in liquid as possible. Simmer, stirring occasionally, until the noodles are just tender and the sauce has thickened slightly, 20 to 25 minutes (add water as needed if the noodles have absorbed all the liquid before they're cooked). Taste and season with salt as needed.

- Remove the pan from the heat and sprinkle with the cheese. Cover and let sit until the cheese is melted, about 4 minutes. Sprinkle with the cilantro and serve.

RECIPE NOTES

Salsa choice: Salsa is important here since it's the foundation of the sauce. Choose a blended salsa and stay away from very dry pico de gallos so that there's plenty of liquid to cook the lasagna noodles. Choose mild or hot salsa depending on your desired spice level.

Vegetarian option: This lasagna can be made vegetarian. Skip the chorizo and use vegetable broth instead of chicken broth.

Go easy on the salt: Since there are a lot of pre-seasoned ingredients in this recipe (chorizo, salsa, broth, and canned beans).

15. How To Make the Best Tomato Grilled Cheese

Sometimes it's the simple pleasures that are the best, like this tomato grilled cheese. Your cast iron pan plays a key role in getting the sandwich just right.

INGREDIENTS

- 1 small loaf hearty country-style bread

- 4 ounces grated cheddar cheese (about 1 cup)

- 4 ounces grated Gruyère cheese (about 1 cup)

- 1 large tomato

- 1/4 cup mayonnaise

- 2 tablespoons unsalted butter, divided

EQUIPMENT

- Box grater

- Bowl

- Cast iron or broiler-safe frying pan

- Serrated knife

- Flat spatula

- Paper towels

INSTRUCTIONS

- Slice the bread: Using a serrated knife, cut 4 (1/2-inch-thick) slices from the center of the loaf. Save the rest of the bread for another use. Mix the cheddar and Gruyère together in a small bowl and set aside.

• Prepare the tomato: Thinly slice the tomato. Use a spoon to remove the watery pulp from the slices. Lay the tomatoes on a paper towel, blot the slices with more paper towels, and set aside on the paper towels while you prepare the rest of the sandwich.

• Heat the broiler: Position a rack about 8 inches below the broiling element, and heat the broiler to medium.

• Toast the bread: Melt 1 tablespoon of the butter in a 12-inch cast iron skillet or broiler-safe frying pan over medium-high heat. Swirl the pan to coat the pan evenly with butter, then add 2 slices of the bread. Fry (that's right — I said fry) until golden-brown on the bottom, 2 to 3 minutes. Transfer the slices to a wire cooling rack. Repeat with the remaining butter and bread slices.

• Spread on mayo: Spread a thin layer of mayonnaise on the unbuttered side of each slice of bread. You might not use all of the mayo.

• Broil the cheese: Give the pan a quick wipe with a paper towel. Place 2 slices of bread back into the pan, buttered-side down. Sprinkle 1/4 of the cheese mixture (about 1/2 cup) over each slice of bread. Broil until melted, 1 to 2 minutes.

- Add the tomato slices: Carefully remove the pan from the broiler and add 2 slices of tomato to each sandwich. Sprinkle with the remaining cheese. Broil again for 1 to 2 minutes.

- Squish and slice: Remove the pan from the oven and top each sandwich with another slice of bread (toasted-side up). Press down on the sandwich with the back of a flat spatula to press the sandwich together. Transfer the sandwiches to a cutting board and cut in half crosswise. Serve immediately.

16. Veggie Burgers

We're not lying when we call these the best-ever veggie burgers. Inspired by a menu item at Northstar Cafe in Columbus, Ohio, the secret to making these taste so good is a combination of beets, black beans, and brown rice.

INGREDIENTS

- 3 large red beets (about 1 pound)

- 1/2 cup brown rice (not cooked)

- 1 medium yellow onion, diced small

123

- 3 to 4 cloves garlic, minced

- 2 tablespoons cider vinegar

- 1/4 cup old-fashioned rolled oats (gluten-free, if necessary)

- 2 (15.5-ounce) cans black beans

- 1/4 cup prunes, chopped into small pieces

- 1 tablespoon extra-virgin olive oil

- 2 to 3 teaspoons smoked paprika, to taste

- 2 teaspoons brown mustard

- 1 teaspoon cumin

- 1/2 teaspoon coriander

- 1/2 teaspoon dried thyme

- 1 large egg (optional, leave out for vegan burgers)

- Salt and pepper

To serve:

- Thin slices of provolone or monterey jack cheese (optional for non-vegan burgers)

- 6 hamburger buns

INSTRUCTIONS

- First, cook the beets: Heat the oven to 400°F. Wrap the beets loosely in aluminum foil and roast until easily pierced with a fork, 50 to 60 minutes. Set aside to cool.

• Cook the rice while the beets roast: Meanwhile, bring a 2-quart pot of water to a boil. Salt the water generously and add the rice. Reduce the heat to a simmer and cook the rice until it's a little beyond al dente. You want it a little over-cooked, but still firm (not completely mushy). This should take about 35 to 40 minutes. Drain the rice and set it aside to cool.

• Begin sautéing the onions when you're done with the rice (or during, if you're OK with multitasking!): Heat a teaspoon of olive oil in a skillet over medium-high heat. Add the onions and a pinch of salt. Stir the onions every minute or two, and cook until they are golden and getting charred around the edges, 10 to 12 minutes. A few wisps of smoke as you are cooking are OK, but if it seems like the onions are burning, lower the heat. A dark, sticky crust should develop on the bottom of the pan.Add the garlic and cook until it is fragrant, about 30 seconds. Pour in the cider vinegar and scrape up the dark sticky crust. Continue to simmer until the cider has evaporated and the pan is nearly dry again. Remove from heat and set aside to cool.

•   Process the oats in a food processor until they have reduced to a fine flour. Transfer to a small bowl and set aside.

•   Drain and rinse one of the cans of beans and transfer the beans to the food processor. Scatter the prunes on top. Pulse in 1-second bursts just until the beans are roughly chopped — not so long that they become mush — 8 to 10 pulses. Transfer this mixture to a large mixing bowl. Drain and rinse the second can of beans and add these whole beans to the mixing bowl as well.

• Grate the roasted beets: Use the edge of a spoon or a paper towel to scrape the skins off the cooled roasted beets; the skins should slip off easily. Grate the peeled beets on the largest holes of a box grater. Transfer the beet gratings to a strainer set over the sink. Press and squeeze the beet gratings to remove as much liquid as possible from the beets. (You can also do this over a bowl and save the beet juice for another purpose.)

- Combine the veggie burger mix:
Transfer the squeezed beets, cooked
rice, and sautéed onions to the bowl with
the beans. Sprinkle the olive oil, brown
mustard, 2 teaspoons of smoked
paprika, cumin, coriander, and thyme
over the top of the mixture. Mix all the
ingredients until combined. Taste the
mixture and add salt, pepper, or any
additional spices or flavorings to taste.
Finally, add the oatmeal flour and egg (if
using — it helps hold everything
together, but isn't 100% necessary), and
mix until you no longer see any dry
oatmeal or egg.

- Refrigerate the burger mix 2 hours, or up to 3 days: Cover the bowl with plastic wrap or transfer the mixture to a refrigerator container, and refrigerate the burger mixture for at least 2 hours or (ideally) overnight. The mix can also be kept refrigerated for up to three days before cooking.

- Shape the burgers: When ready to cook the burgers, first shape them into burgers. Scoop up about a scant cup of the burger mixture and shape it between your palms into a thick patty the size of your hamburger buns. You should end up with 6 large patties.

- Cook the burgers: Heat a cast iron skillet over high heat. Add a few tablespoons of vegetable oil to completely coat the bottom of the pan. When you see the oil shimmer and a flick of water evaporates on contact, the pan is ready.Transfer the patties to the pan. Cook as many as will fit without crowding; I normally cook 3 patties at a time in my 10-inch cast iron skillet.Cook the patties for 2 minutes, then flip them to the other side. You should see a nice crust on the cooked side. If any pieces break off when you flip the burgers, just pat them back into place with the spatula. Cook for another 2 minutes, then cover the pan and reduce the heat to medium-low. Cook for 4 more minutes until the patties are warmed through. If you're adding cheese, lay a slice over the burgers in the last minute of cooking.Serve the veggie burgers on soft burger buns or lightly toasted sandwich bread along with some fresh greens.

RECIPE NOTES

Freezing Burgers: Burgers can be frozen raw or cooked. Wrap each burger individually in plastic or between sheets of parchment paper, and freeze. Raw burgers are best if thawed in the fridge overnight before cooking. Cooked burgers can be reheated in the oven, a toaster oven, or the microwave.

Grilling Burgers: While I haven't had a chance to try grilling these burgers, they are firm enough to do well on a grill, particularly if you cook them in a grill pan or other device. You may also want to add an egg to the mix to help the burgers hold together better.

Making Your Own Beans: Northstar makes their own black beans for their burgers. If you would like to do this, try cooking your beans with an onion, a clove or two of garlic, and some dried

ancho or chipotle chile peppers for extra
flavor.

Made in United States
Orlando, FL
21 November 2021

10613192R00075